Flowchart Science

LIGHT

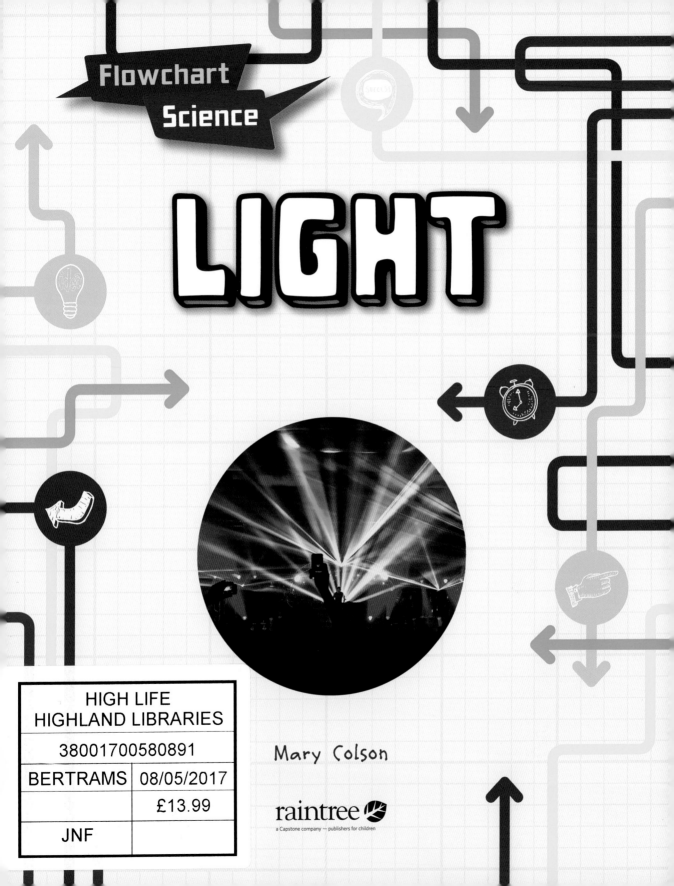

Mary Colson

raintree
a Capstone company — publishers for children

Raintree is an imprint of Capstone Global Library Limited, a company incorporated in England and Wales having its registered office at 264 Banbury Road, Oxford OX2 7DY – Registered company number: 6695582

www.raintree.co.uk
myorders@raintree.co.uk

Text © Capstone Global Library Limited 2017
The moral rights of the proprietor have been asserted.

Produced for Raintree by Calcium
Edited by Sarah Eason and Amanda Learmonth
Designed by Simon Borrough
Picture research by Susannah Jayes
Production by Victoria Fitzgerald
Originated by Capstone Global Library Ltd © 2016
Printed and bound in China

ISBN 978 1 4747 3128 7
20 19 18 17 16
10 9 8 7 6 5 4 3 2 1

British Library Cataloguing in Publication Data
A full catalogue record for this book is available from the British Library

Acknowledgements
We would like to thank the following for permission to reproduce photographs: NASA: KIPAC/SLAC/M. Alvarez, T. Abel and J. Wise, 40–41; Shutterstock: Aptyp KoK 35tr, Beboy 6–7, Bikeriderlondon 38–39, John A. Davis 4–5b, Drop of Light 19, Erkki & Hanna 38, Kellie L. Folkerts 24–25, Piotr Krzeslak 8t, Mubus7 34–35, Gianluca D. Muscelli 40, Robert Neumann 28–29, PanatFoto 45, Phatic Photography 12–13, Pikselstock 32–33, M. Pilot 18–19, Dr Morley Read 14–15, Fouad A. Saad 29, Vladimir Salman 13, Ivan Smuk 20–21, Solarseven 8b, Somchaiito 8–9, Ssuaphotos 32, Szefei 34b, Triff 4–5t, Pavel Tvrdy 26–27, Wavebreakmedia 26, Zhykova 1, 44–45.

Cover art reproduced with permission of: Shutterstock: Denkcreative, Lineartestpilot.

Every effort has been made to contact copyright holders of material reproduced in this book. Any omissions will be rectified in subsequent printings if notice is given to the publisher.

Contents

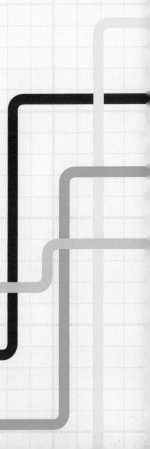

Chapter 1

What is light?

Light is essential for all life on Earth to exist. It can travel faster than anything else that we know about in the whole universe. Light cannot be heard, tasted, touched or smelt. We see the effects of light when it bounces off other objects and enters our eyes.

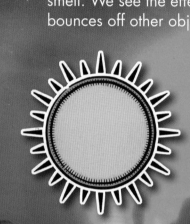

The Sun is our planet's star. It takes around 8 minutes for light from the surface of the Sun to reach Earth.

The *aurora borealis* is a natural light display that can be seen in some northern parts of the planet.

Light is an energy source. Most of the light on Earth comes from the Sun. Think about how you are reading this book right now. You might be using daylight, electric light or a mixture of natural and **artificial** light. You could be using a lamp, a torch or a candle. These are all light sources and without them, life wouldn't just be very different, it would be impossible.

The study of light is a type of physics called optics. "Optics" comes from a Greek word meaning "visible". This book explores what light is, where it comes from, what colours are within it, what light has to do with sight and how it acts. We will also look at how humans, animals and plants use light to survive.

Get smart!

The Sun is Earth's **primary** light source. It is much bigger than Earth and it is the centre of our solar system. At more than 1,368,000 kilometres (850,000 miles) wide, it is more than 100 times wider than Earth. The Sun's surface temperature is 5,500 degrees Celsius (9,940 degrees Fahrenheit) but its core is many times hotter at around 13.6 million degrees Celsius (24.4 million degrees Fahrenheit). **Molecules** of helium and hydrogen gas crash together in its core, which produces light energy and heat. All stars produce light in this way. Sunlight and heat are essential for life on Earth.

Objects that give us light

Objects that give out light are called **luminous** objects. The Sun, stars, candles, fire and electric lights are all luminous. Animals that create their own light are called **bioluminescent**. In the natural world, fireflies and glow-worms use a chemical reaction inside their own bodies to create light. In the ocean, some types of squid, sea stars and plankton create light to attract mates and warn off **predators**. All other objects are **non-luminous**, which means that they do not produce their own light. We see these objects because they reflect light. For example, the Moon is non-luminous. It acts like a giant mirror, reflecting light from the Sun.

Think about your home and all the various ways you can create light in different rooms. Artificial light is created by electricity. Look around you now. If you are at school or in a library, there are probably electric lights to help you see and read. Some materials are **fluorescent**. These glow when certain forms of energy, such as a flow of electrons, passes through them. Long, tube-shaped light bulbs often found in schools are fluorescent bulbs. They contain a gas that glows when the electricity is switched on. Televisions and mobile phone screens are also light sources.

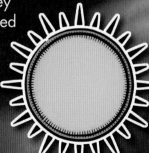

Light is also created when we light a candle or a fire. Burning happens when a substance combines rapidly with oxygen in the air. Lighting a candle or a gas fire involves a chemical change that produces light energy. Think about striking a match. Before it is struck, there is no light. The match is non-luminous. But when you strike it, it burns and it mixes with oxygen to produce light. Like most light sources, it also creates heat.

Artificial light allows us to be active after the Sun has set when there is less natural light.

Moving light

Light is made up of tiny packets of energy called **photons**. An empty space is called a vacuum, and in a vacuum photons travel incredibly quickly in straight, parallel lines. However, we do not live in a vacuum. On Earth, light does not always travel at the same speed and in the same direction, and it cannot pass through all objects.

The bending of light is called **refraction**. When light passes through water it slows down and bends. This is because water is denser than air. Put a pencil in a glass of water and lean it to one side. Now look through the side of the glass. The pencil will look as though it is bent.

Water is a **transparent** material, which means that light can pass through it. Glass and air are also transparent materials. The book you are reading right now is **opaque**. Light does not pass through opaque materials – instead, they reflect and absorb light.

The seas and oceans of Earth act like giant mirrors that reflect some of the Sun's light.

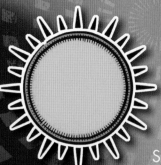

Shadows form when light is blocked by an opaque object. Your body is an opaque object and on a sunny day it blocks the light beams and a shadow forms on the ground. Your shadow has the same shape as you because the light beams are travelling in straight lines.

Light cannot pass through objects such as trees.

Shadows are areas where there is less light.

Get smart!

Light travels at an incredible 300,000 kilometres (186,000 miles) per second. Light from the Sun takes about 8 minutes to reach Earth. Light from other stars takes years to reach us, because they are much further away than our Sun. Some stars are so distant that their light is still travelling to Earth even though the stars themselves have stopped shining. **Astronomers** measure distance in light years, which is how far a beam of light travels in one year.

Get flowchart smart!

How light travels

Let's take a look at how light travels, using a flowchart.

Light is made up of tiny particles called photons. These are packets of energy.

Superhot helium and hydrogen molecules fuse in the core of the Sun and create light.

Light cannot pass through opaque objects, which creates shadows.

Billions of photons create light waves. These travel rapidly from the Sun, through the vacuum of space, in straight lines.

When light waves try to travel through different materials on Earth, such as water, glass or stone, they slow down, bend or are absorbed.

When light waves change speed, they bend.

Flowchart
Smart

Chapter 2
Light and sight

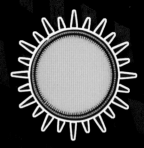

Light allows you to see the world around you. You can read the words on this page because light is coming from a light source. The book is not producing light, but light from a lamp or the Sun is reflecting from the book and into your eyes.

Absolutely everything you can see is a result of light that has travelled from an object into your eyes. Eyes control the amount of light that enters them. When you enter a dark room, your eyes take a few moments to adjust and enable you to see properly. The eye muscles in your **iris** open the pupil to let in more light. In very bright places, the iris closes the pupil so that only a small amount of light can enter.

Eyes located on the front of the head are able to judge distance. Light from an object reaches and enters one eye slightly before it enters the other eye. This slight difference allows us to work out how far away something is and in which direction it is moving. This is useful for animals that hunt their own food.

The pupil is a hole in the iris that allows light to enter the eye.

Human eyes have two sets of muscles in the iris: radial and circular muscles. Together, they look like a bicycle wheel. When you move from a lighter place to a darker one, the radial muscles pull. This makes your pupil larger. When you move from a darker to a lighter place, the circular muscles pull and your pupil gets smaller. The light travels to the back of the eye to the retina. There, it makes an upside-down image. The information about the image is sent along the optic nerve to the brain where it is decoded and turned the right way up.

The iris controls how much light enters our eyes.

Seeing in the dark

At any one time, half of planet Earth is in darkness. Humans cannot see in total darkness, but if there is even a little light, our eyes can adjust so we are able to see something. We "see" the world by collecting light in our eyes and when there is no light, we think of it as dark.

When it is dark, humans mostly see in different shades of grey. Scientists have now discovered that some **nocturnal** animals, such as bats, moths and geckos, have colour vision even in near-total darkness. This is because their eyes have larger lenses that allow them to detect colours in light that human eyes cannot see.

Get smart!

During World War II, German bombers targeted British cities under cover of darkness. The Royal Air Force [RAF] managed to fight back because they had developed top-secret radar equipment. To keep the new technology secret, the British government said that their pilots could see in the dark because they ate a lot of carrots, which are rich in vitamin A. It is known that low levels of vitamin A can cause night blindness but scientists are yet to agree that eating carrots improves your general sight.

Nocturnal animals also have very large pupils. This allows as much light as possible to enter the eye. The tarsier, an animal that lives in the Southeast Asian rainforests, has eyes that each weigh more than its brain. It has the largest eyes relative to its body size of any mammal on Earth. If human eyes were like the tarsier's, our eyes would be the size of grapefruits!

Alligators, crocodiles and caimans are nocturnal animals. They can see well in the dark, which helps them hunt under water and at night.

Get flowchart smart!

How our eyes see light

Follow the flowchart to understand how our eyes capture or "see" light.

The iris is the coloured part of your eye and it controls the amount of light that enters the eye.

The pupil is the hole in the iris. It lets light into the eye and changes size depending on how bright the surroundings are.

The brain decodes the information and we "see" the image the right way up.

Light hits the lens behind the pupil. The lens focuses the light onto the retina at the back of the eye.

→

The retina "records" an upside-down image of the object the eye is looking at.

When an image forms, thousands of nerve endings send electric signals from the retina, along the optic nerve, to the brain. The signals carry information about the colour and brightness of the light.

Flowchart
Smart

Chapter 3

Light and colour

Physicists call light from the Sun "white light". White light contains all of the colours of light. All objects also have a colour. Each of us might see these colours slightly differently, but all the colours are present and the way we see them depends on light.

When white light strikes an object, the colours in the light are reflected or absorbed. If all the colours in white light are reflected, we see the object as white. If all the colours are absorbed, we see the object as black. Look around at the objects near you now. If there is a red object, it looks red because the object has absorbed all the colours in white light except red, which it has reflected. Every colour you can see is what is being reflected from white light.

The colour of an object is what we see when the rest of the colours in white light have been absorbed.

Get smart!

In order to see colour, we have rod and cone cells in our retinas. Rods can "see" black and white, and cones can "see" colours. There are different cones for detecting red, blue and green. To see colours properly, we need all three types of cones. If the cones do not work or are missing, the brain does not get the right information about what colours are being viewed. This means that a colour-blind person will not see green when they look at grass but perhaps will see grey instead.

Scientists call the white light that humans can see "**visible** light". The photons that make up visible light have different wavelengths. A light wave vibrates up and down and the wavelength is the distance between two peaks of the wave. The longest waves look red to the human eye and the shortest waves look violet. All colours are produced by different light wavelengths.

Every different shade of colour we see has a different wavelength.

Electromagnetic spectrum

Visible light is made up of seven different colours: red, orange, yellow, green, blue, indigo and violet. These colours are the light waves that the human eye can detect. Visible light is part of a much bigger range of waves, called the electromagnetic spectrum. Humans cannot detect most of the wavelengths in this spectrum.

Infrared cameras take pictures that show the different levels of heat in objects. Red and orange indicate warm areas; blue and green indicate colder areas.

There are many different types of waves in the electromagnetic spectrum including radio waves, microwaves, infrared (IR) rays, ultraviolet (UV) rays and X-rays. Infrared rays are found beyond red at one end of the visible spectrum and ultraviolet (UV) waves are found beyond violet at the other end of the spectrum. "Ultra" means "beyond", while "infra" means "below". IR rays come from all objects around us, including our own bodies, and you can feel IR waves as warmth on your skin. UV light is what causes skin to tan in sunny weather. Both IR and UV waves can be harmful to humans if we are overexposed to them. Some animals can detect IR and UV waves. Birds and bees use UV waves to **navigate** and see. Some snakes have special organs in their heads to detect IR waves. This helps them sense warmth from their **prey** when it is too dark to see visible light.

Get smart!

The air around us is full of dust and tiny gas molecules. When light from the Sun passes through these, it bounces off in different directions. Some colours of light, like red and orange, pass straight through the air, but some of the blue light in light waves is bent or scattered. This is what makes the sky appear blue. In a similar way, when white light enters a cloud, water droplets scatter it in all directions. This makes the cloud appear white.

Get flowchart smart!

Light's colours

Follow the flowchart to discover how white light can be separated into its different colours and wavelengths.

White light is made up of photons, which all have different wavelengths.

In this refraction, white light separates into its different colours. This dispersion produces a rainbow effect.

Each wavelength of light forms a different colour. At one end of the visible light spectrum, red has a long wavelength. At the other end, violet light has a shorter wavelength.

When light passes through a glass, water, a gemstone or a **prism**, the light waves are refracted, or bent.

Because light waves have different wavelengths, each wavelength is refracted at a slightly different angle.

Flowchart Smart

Chapter 4

Light and mirrors

Mirrors are used to see reflected images. Most objects, such as a carpet or a page in a book, have rough surfaces that reflect light waves in many different directions. You cannot see your reflection in these objects. Mirrors have very smooth, shiny surfaces and reflect light in an even way. It looks as though there is an object behind the mirror.

Light travels in a straight line and hits the surface of a mirror at a certain angle. This is called the angle of incidence. On a smooth surface, light bounces back off at the same angle in straight, **parallel** lines. This means that the light rays stay together and do not spread out. The path the light takes away from the mirror's surface is called the angle of reflection. Because the light is reflected in a single direction, we can see a reflected image. The image that is created is called a specular reflection.

If the surface of the mirror is not completely smooth, the light rays will not bounce off at the same angle or in parallel lines. The rays scatter and the reflected image will be distorted. This is a diffuse reflection.

Get smart!

A mirror image is a reflection of an object that looks exactly the same as the original but is reversed. This means that the left and right sides of an image are reflections of each other. This is also called reflection symmetry. If you are looking at a mirror image of a face, there will be a line of symmetry between the two images or two halves.

Funfair mirrors distort light rays. This is because light hits the mirror in different places and is reflected from the surface in different directions.

Mirrors

Mirrors need smooth surfaces to reflect light, but they are not always flat. There are three different types of smooth mirror that are used in different ways in daily life. These are plane mirrors, convex mirrors and concave mirrors.

Plane mirrors are flat and are most commonly used in the home to look at our own reflection. They are also used in telescopes, cameras and microscopes. They can be used to make **periscopes** for submarines or to help people see above a crowd at a big event. In a device like a kaleidoscope, more than one plane mirror is used to reflect light and create amazing reflections. Solar panels use plane mirrors to reflect sunlight to a point in the panel where the light energy can be collected. Plane mirrors can also be used to protect us from sunlight. Mirrored sunglasses use plane mirrors to reflect light away from our eyes.

Scientists use plane mirrors in microscopes to reflect light onto tiny organisms.

Concave and convex mirrors have a smooth but curved surface. Concave mirrors curve inwards. They bend light inwards and focus light to a point. Dentists use concave mirrors to focus light on the area of the mouth they are looking at. Concave mirrors make a reflection appear bigger than the original object. Convex mirrors bulge outwards and bend light outwards. A convex mirror makes the reflection appear smaller than in real life.

Cars' mirrors are convex to help drivers see behind them. Hold up a teaspoon to see your reflection in the concave side. What do you notice? The curved surface is a concave mirror so your reflection will be upside down. The spoon is concave, so the light goes in and out of the mirror at an angle. Now look at your reflection in the convex side of the spoon. How does the image appear now? Why might the reflection be different?

Mirrors in huge telescopes help astronomers see far into distant space.

Lenses

A lens is a piece of curved transparent material that either focuses or disperses light rays. Lenses are used to help humans see more clearly, and they are also used in photography.

The lenses in our eyes bend light so that it focuses directly on the retina. If a person has trouble with their vision it is often because their eyes do not bend the light correctly. Lenses in glasses or contact lenses correct this. They refract the light onto the retina so that a clear image is formed.

Telescopes and binoculars use convex lenses to bend light rays to a single point to help our eyes focus on distant objects. The focal length is a measure of the strength or power of a lens. This is the distance from the middle of the lens to the point at which it focuses light rays. Magnifying glasses also use convex lenses.

Cameras use lenses and mirrors to allow light to reach the sensor and record a photograph. Photograph means "light image".

A pinhole camera is a simple camera without a lens. A small hole lets light in and an inverted image is created, just like in our eyes.

In a Single Lens Reflex (SLR) camera, light enters the lens and is reflected to the viewfinder using mirrors. There is a slanted mirror with a prism or another mirror above it located between the shutter and the lens. The first mirror creates an **inverted** image and the second mirror or prism turns it up the right way so it can be seen correctly in the viewfinder. When you take a photograph, the first mirror is moved out of the way so that light can reach the camera film. This captures the image. In a digital camera, the lens focuses light on a sensor made out of silicon. The sensor contains millions of pixels that are sensitive to light. Together, the pixels create a picture from the light they receive and this is the image that we see on screen.

Get flowchart smart!

29

Light and mirrors

Using a flowchart, let's take a look at how light travels towards and away from a mirror.

Light waves strike the smooth surface of a mirror. This is the angle of incidence.

Because the mirror is smooth and shiny, it reflects the waves. They bounce off at the same angle in parallel lines. This is the angle of reflection.

The result is called a specular reflection and the image you see is a true image.

If the surface of a mirror is not perfectly smooth, the light waves bounce off at different angles. This is a diffuse reflection and the image you see is wobbly and distorted.

SUCCESS

Flowchart
Smart

Chapter 5
How do we use light energy?

For thousands of years, humans have been using the light and heat of the Sun to grow crops, dry and preserve food, and dry clothes. Today, technological advances have resulted in many new applications in our homes and our workplaces for light energy.

A laser is an intense, narrow beam of light that, unlike ordinary light, stays focused to a point. The light rays do not spread out. Laser beams are used for cutting steel, burning marks into metal, reading barcodes and in place of a blade in eye surgery.

Scientists are discovering new ways of using light all the time, such as using UV light to whiten teeth.

Beyond the visible spectrum, there are a lot of uses for other electromagnetic waves. Microwaves are used in cooking appliances and radio waves are used for communication. Any object that gives out heat produces infrared **radiation**. Security cameras can detect infrared waves, which allow them to "see" in the dark. The police and the army also use infrared detection devices to locate criminals or the enemy. In science and medicine, X-rays are used to form images of human bones and gamma rays are used to treat cancers.

We use solar panels to collect energy from light rays.

Get smart!

Every day, all over the world, we use huge amounts of electricity. Every time you turn on a light, a television or a computer, you use electricity. When you turn on a lamp, electrons move through the cord and light the bulb. This flow of electrons is called electricity. A solar panel turns the Sun's light into electricity. Each panel is made up of solar cells. These cells use light to make electrons move and create a flow of electricity. This can then be used to power homes, cars and even remote scientific research stations in places such as Antarctica, where for six months of the year there is constant sunlight.

Using light to make food

Plants use light energy from the Sun in a process called photosynthesis. In Greek, "photo" means "light" and "synthesis" means "putting together". During photosynthesis, plants use light energy to turn water and carbon dioxide into food and oxygen. Animals breathe out carbon dioxide into the atmosphere. Plants take in this carbon dioxide and produce oxygen. Animals breathe in the oxygen that plants produce. As a result, plants and animals, including humans, are dependent on each other for life.

Inside a plant's cells are structures called chloroplasts, which contain a pigment called chlorophyll. This green pigment absorbs the Sun's energy and uses it to convert water and carbon dioxide into a sugar called glucose. Green plants use the glucose as food to grow.

In forests, plants compete for sunlight. Their leaves turn towards the Sun to maximize photosynthesis.

Plant cells capture sunlight in chloroplasts. Inside these, a chemical called chlorophyll converts sunlight into energy for growth.

Get smart!

Euglena is a microscopic, unique organism that lives in water. It has only one cell but this cell contains chloroplasts. This means it can conduct photosynthesis and make food using light, just like a plant. It can also eat food like an animal.

Amazingly, there are some animals on Earth that manage to survive with either little or no light at all. Deep-ocean organisms live thousands of metres below the surface of the water. This is the aphotic ("without light") zone and it is a harsh place to live. There is very little oxygen or food, no sunlight and it is extremely cold. Photosynthesis is impossible there because there is not enough light. The creatures that live at these depths, such as the giant isopod, have adapted to the conditions. Their body processes are slow and they can go for months or even years without food. When they do eat, they feed on both live and dead animals including fish, crab, squid and sponges.

Get flowchart smart!

Photosynthesis

Follow the flowchart for a close look at photosynthesis.

Sunlight shines on a green plant's leaves and a chemical compound called chlorophyll absorbs light energy.

A green plant takes in water through its roots and carbon dioxide through its leaves.

The plant stores some of the food to use during months when there is less sunlight.

The plant changes water and carbon dioxide into a sugar called glucose using the Sun's energy.

The plant uses glucose as food. It gives the plant energy to grow. The plant also releases oxygen into the atmosphere.

The chemical equation for photosynthesis is: carbon dioxide + water

$$\text{carbon dioxide} + \text{water} \xrightarrow{\text{Sun's energy} + \text{chlorophyll}} \text{glucose} + \text{oxygen}.$$

Flowchart
Smart

Chapter 6
Losing light

We live in such a light-drenched world that it is easy to forget that much of the light around us is man-made. In the future, as more of Earth's population has access to electricity, we are likely to produce even more artificial light. What does the future hold for the Sun and other light sources?

The Sun is a star like any other we see in the night sky. One day the Sun, like all stars, will eventually stop shining. Billions of years from now, our star will start to run out of hydrogen. When this happens, it will expand. This will affect life on Earth in many ways. It will change the chemical balance of our atmosphere and photosynthesis will no longer be possible. It will cause Earth's surface temperature to increase and most life on our planet will become extinct. When the Sun finally goes dark, its light will still travel through space for many millions of years.

We have adjusted to living with light. People who live in very sunny places, such as Bedouins of the Middle East, wear black clothes to help keep cool. The black clothing absorbs heat, keeping it away from the skin. Will we adjust so well if our planet begins to lose the light and heat of the Sun?

People who live in remote regions near the North Pole adjust their lives to living in the cold and with little light for six months of the year.

Get smart!

The greenhouse effect is leading to the gradual warming of planet Earth. This effect is caused by an increase in greenhouse gases, such as carbon dioxide, in the air. Greenhouse gases trap light energy from the Sun and prevent it from bouncing back into space. This leads to the planet getting hotter and is called global warming. Many scientists believe that global warming is causing the planet's climate to change. The rise in the average temperature of the Earth's atmosphere and its oceans is causing more extreme weather patterns around the world. For example, droughts are lasting longer in some places, making it impossible to grow enough food there.

Light in space

We tend to think of space as being a dark place where there is no light. The light in space comes from stars. The planets and moons of the solar systems reflect starlight out into space. When you look at the night sky, you can see many stars, particularly if you are in the countryside and away from the **light pollution** of a city.

From space, much of our planet is lit up at night by artificial light, or light pollution. Dark Sky sites are places around the world where there is less light pollution. At these locations, the thousands of stars in the night sky can be seen.

Black holes are the only known places in the whole universe where there is no light at all.

Some stars are thousands or even millions of times brighter than our Sun. The brightness of a star is called its magnitude. Sometimes, **comets** are visible in the night sky. Comets are balls of ice and dust that orbit a star. They travel across space, with "tails" of gas and dust streaming out from them. Meteors are lumps of rock and metal that hit Earth's outer atmosphere and burn up, leaving bright streaks of light across the night sky. These are called shooting stars. When the Earth passes through a comet tail it is possible to see a meteor shower, in which hundreds of shooting stars light up the night sky.

Get smart!

A black hole is a place in the universe that light cannot enter or escape from. It is a place so unique that it cannot even be seen. A black hole is a region of space where matter has collapsed in on itself. Black holes form when a large star has used up all its gases and can no longer support its own weight. The black hole that is created by the star's collapse is an area of extreme high pressure. The pull of gravity in a black hole is so great that nothing can escape, not even light. Scientists know that black holes exist from the way that nearby dust, stars and galaxies are affected.

Get flowchart smart!

Solar eclipse

A solar eclipse occurs when the Moon briefly blocks the Sun's light. Follow the flowchart for a closer look at how a solar eclipse occurs. Remember, if you watch a solar eclipse, you must wear special solar eclipse glasses. Never look directly at the Sun.

When the Moon passes directly between the Sun and Earth, it blocks some of the Sun's light.

This casts a shadow on Earth and, gradually, the sky gets darker.

As the Moon continues to move, the Sun starts to reappear. It becomes lighter and warmer again on Earth.

From Earth, it looks as though the Moon is taking a bite out of the Sun.

The Moon moves across the Sun until just a small crescent of light can be seen.

The sky darkens when the Sun is totally eclipsed by the Moon. All that is visible is a thin ring of the Sun's light around the edge of the Moon. The air feels colder.

Flowchart Smart

The light fantastic!

Light is the key to all life on Earth. Without light, there can be no photosynthesis in plants and without plants, humans and other animals could not survive. We would not be able to see and Earth would be a cold and empty place. We have discovered how light is Earth's most important **resource**, but it is under threat.

We know that at some point, the Sun itself will stop shining. However, scientists think the biggest problem facing humans now is what to do about the trapping of the Sun's energy inside our atmosphere. It is impossible to predict exactly what will happen if Earth's climate changes significantly, but it could mean more extreme weather events, rising sea levels, freshwater shortages, crop failure and disease outbreaks.

Get smart!

As more countries of the world become developed, there is an increasing need for more artificial light. Energy-efficient light bulbs are being developed to illuminate our future homes, towns and cities. Light-emitting diodes (LEDs) are electronic lights that can last for 80,000 hours, 10 times longer than ordinary bulbs. Energy-efficient lights, other energy-efficient machines and the use of **renewable energy** such as solar energy will all help reduce the greenhouse effect and hopefully prevent climate change.

Lasers can be used to create spectacular light shows, but we need to learn how to manage our precious light resources in a sustainable way.

For centuries, scientists and engineers have marvelled at the power and possibilities of light energy. They have harnessed it to make artificial light and energy to power our daily lives. Solar power stations gather sunlight and transform it into electricity. Lasers can cut through sheet metal and assist in delicate surgical procedures. Mirrors and lenses can be used to angle light to help people in their jobs, whether they are photographers, dentists or submariners. The uses are endless.

In the future, more and more artificial light may be used to power our lives.

Glossary

artificial made by people, not natural

astronomer scientist who studies space, stars and planets

bioluminescent able to produce light naturally as a living thing

comet ball of rock and ice that orbits a star

fluorescent producing a bright light when a certain type of energy, such as a flow of electrons, is applied to it

gravity force of attraction between two or more objects with mass

inverted upside down

iris coloured part of the eye that controls the amount of light let in

light pollution unwanted or harmful artificial light that limits observations of the night sky

luminous giving out light

matter material substance that makes up everything in the universe; matter occupies space and has mass

molecule the smallest unit of a substance that has all the characteristics of that substance

navigate follow a course to get from one place to another

nocturnal active only at night

non-luminous not able to produce light

opaque blocking all rays of light

parallel same distance apart at all points; parallel lines never meet

periscope device used in a submarine that allows the sailors inside the vessel to see what is happening above the water

photon tiny particle of light

physicist scientist who studies matter and energy

predator animal that hunts other animals

prey animal that is eaten by other animals for food

primary first or main

prism solid transparent object with internal refracting surfaces that can separate white light into the colour spectrum

radiation energy from electromagnetic waves

refraction change in direction of a wave of light when it enters a different material

remote far away and difficult to reach

renewable energy form of energy made from a source that can be replaced or used again

resource supply of something useful, such as water, air and fuel

retina membrane lining the back of the eyeball

transparent allowing all rays of light to pass through it

visible allowing all rays of light to pass

Find out more

Books

Killer Energy (Horrible Science), Nick Arnold (Scholastic, 2014)

Light and Colour (Straight Forward with Science), Peter Riley (Franklin Watts, 2015)

Science (DKfindout!), Emily Grossman (Dorling Kindersley, 2016)

Our Universe (Infographic How It Works) John Richards (Wayland, 2016)

Websites

Watch this video to see how light travels in straight lines:
www.bbc.co.uk/education/clips/zyntsbk

Discover more about animals that can produce light:
www.dkfindout.com/uk/science/light/animals-that-produce-light/

Try out some cool experiments about light at this website:
www.easyscienceexperiments.co.uk/making-light-work-science/

Read some fascinating facts about stars and stargazing:
www.nationaltrust.org.uk/features/mind-boggling-facts-about-stargazing-for-kids

Index